# Chowder Summer: One Man Eats Rhode Island, Manhattan and New England (And Still Has Room for Oyster Crackers)

DAVID NORTON STONE

To

My Father

On the Fourth of July, 1840, the biggest all male

chowder party in the history of the world was held at

Buttonwoods in Warwick, Rhode Island.  Back then

Buttonwoods was a peaceful campground, later a Baptist

summer colony, and now it is a district of historic

waterfront homes I can see across Greenwich Bay from

an upstairs window of my house if I crane my neck.  The

occasion in the summer of 1840 was a political

convention held by the friends of William Henry

Harrison, a candidate for President of the United States.

An enduring political rivalry with which we are all too unfortunately familiar stirred the chowder pot that year.

I speak, of course, of the bickering between the locofocos and the Whigs. The names have changed but not the dysfunction.

Harrison, a Whig, ran on the born-in-a-log-cabin, hard-cider platform, against the Democrat incumbent Martin Van Buren, whose supporters were known as the locofocos. Maybe from history class you remember Harrison's campaign slogan "Tippecanoe and Tyler Too" in reference to Harrison's victory over the Native Americans at Tippecanoe and to John Tyler, his running mate from Virginia.

Harrison's campaign organizers held rowdy rallies everywhere, but none were as clammy as the one on Independence Day in Buttonwoods.

The people of Rhode Island and neighboring states were invited to attend and to partake in a "clam bake and chowder" served at two o'clock.   The menu was circulated widely beforehand and printed in newspapers:

Fish Chowder,

Roasted Quahogs,

Baked Clams,

Brown and White Bread,

Crackers and Cheese,

Iced Lemonade,

Iced Cider

A ticket to the Chowder and Bake cost fifty cents, and people were asked to oblige the Committee by purchasing tickets early, probably so the organizers could know how much chowder to make. The preparations entailed stockpiling two hundred and twenty bushels of clams, eighty bushels of quahogs, one thousand pounds of brown bread, five hundred pounds of white bread, five barrels of fish for the chowder, fifteen barrels of crackers and pilot bread (also for the chowder) and eight thousand pounds of ice.

A brass band was promised as well as two log-cabins. Eaters could travel via train cars from Providence, on the ship *King Philip* from Fall River and Bristol or another ship the *Balloon* from Newport. Would there be any clams left in Narragansett Bay after this? The Whigs ran the show, but locofocos who could be swayed by the promise of clams were welcome too.

*

It rained on July 3, and the locofocos predicted the Chowder and Bake the following day would be a washout. The Whigs countered that it never rained on the Fourth of July, in general, and certainly wouldn't when five barrels of fish were being chowdered for Harrison.

And the Whigs were right as confirmed by the weather report of the *Providence Journal*. "At 9 o'clock the bright Whig sun came out full in teeth of the locofoco North Easter, and the clouds rolled away as the British and Indians scattered before Harrison at Tippecanoe and Fort Meigs, and as the locofocos will scatter before him next November."

So much for journalistic independence.

It was hard to count just how many people showed up that long ago Fourth of July. Food was prepared for between eight and ten thousand people. Thousands arrived on the streetcars from Providence, and the steamboats were loaded as well. Someone counted forty-three boats in the bay, sloops, schooners, steamboats and sailboats, carrying Whigs to clams. The rain the previous day had cooled the air and washed nature clean. A fresh breeze circulated the smell of roasting clams and scorched rockweed (always rockweed and always scorched for a clambake) and flapped the flags on the log-cabin erected by the Tippecanoe Boys of Coventry's Washington Village. The log cabin acted as a billboard and was decorated with portraits of Washington, John Hancock and Harrison, as well as political slogans. Hard cider was served out of the windows.

Companies of Kentish Guards and Pawtuxet Artillery

drilled and thrilled. But what about the food? It was ready around three o'clock. By four-thirty there was nothing left but clam shells. It was managed ingeniously. There were about eighty heaps of clambakes. Each man brought his own plate, bowl, spoon, knife and fork and helped himself, then sat under the shade of the spreading, mottled-bark Buttonwood trees which gave the area its name.

Never was bread browner, butter sweeter, and cider harder. The hard cider was, in fact, a point of pride, since the temperance preaching locofocos were opposed to this drink, some even going so far as to call Harrison "Old Tip-ler". Even with the hard cider, the rally goers were impeccably behaved.

And never was chowder...fishier. Unfortunately, the clams appear to have been roasted or baked and not cooked in the chowder pot. I suspect that this was a clear chowder since the shopping list did not include tomatoes or milk.

A few days after the event, a man named Charley wrote to the *Providence Journal* and recounted what he related to his wife. "I've been to the bigest clam bake that was ever made in the world;-the bigest in the quantity of clams-the bigest in the quantity of folks to eat 'em-the bigest in good order and rational enjoyment-and finally the bigest all the ways you have a mind to look at it…I never lined my jacket with better clams in all my born days. Them Warwick chaps are the boys to come a clam bake in a syentifick manner…."

Is it me, or is Charley just too quaint a picture of the country farmer, misspellings and all, to be true?

But Charley had to tell his wife about the event

rather than bring her along for an outing, because

women didn't vote and weren't welcome.  So although

this may have been the biggest clambake in history it

cannot be called the best if no women were allowed.  It

is bad enough to deny women the right to vote, but cruel

and unusual punishment to also keep them away from a

good chowder.

And what of Harrison?  Was it all worth it?  He

won the election in November and then, on March 4,

1841, hatless, gloveless, overcoatless, chowderless and

ciderless, delivered a two hour long inaugural address in

dismal, wintery weather.  He was dead within a month

and, until very recently, the cause was attributed to

pneumonia brought on by a chill contracted on

inauguration day.

But according to the book *Diagnosing Giants:*

*Solving the Medical Mysteries of Thirteen Patients Who Changed the World* by Dr. Philip Mackowiak, Harrison may have died from gastroenteritis, brought on by the proximity of the White House to a dumping ground for raw sewage.  To make matters worse, Harrison's doctor treated him in ways that curbed his body's ability to rid itself of the microbial assassins.

Unfortunately, the man who was helped into office by a clam pig-out died of a stomach ailment.

*Forget everything you think you know about chowder.*

I would like to make a grand claim like that but I cannot. This is not a history of chowder, let alone a revisionist one. My goal has simply been to focus on one place, Rhode Island, where clam chowder was, is and always shall be a favored dish. I wanted to discover if an unfortunate regional chauvinism that raises its head in any discussion of clam chowder (and whose justification is "tradition") always existed, or if chowder in the past had the same fluid boundaries it enjoys today.

Frankly, I was tired of hearing that red chowder belongs in Manhattan, white in New England and clear in

Rhode Island.  Such a notion comports with neither my understanding of human nature and tastes nor with my own observations as a life-long resident of Rhode Island, New England and sometimes Manhattan.

I unwittingly contributed to the problem.  The topic of clam chowder came up in my first newspaper interview for a book I wrote about an entirely different clam product, clamcakes.  Perhaps because of my connections to both New York City (where I work during the week) and Rhode Island, where my house is, the interviewer told me a story about his honeymoon in Manhattan.  He and his wife ordered clam chowder and were shocked when bowls of something red emerged from the kitchen instead of creamy and white as they expected.  I suppose the point was that New Yorkers don't know what they're doing when it comes to chowder or, more charitably, that chowder means something different according to where you live.

I was quoted by the reporter as saying the following: "You don't get too much [white] chowder in New York," said Stone. "Unless you specify, you get red."

I may have said this, but it's not what I meant. In fact, my experience is just the opposite. In New York, you don't get too much red chowder. Unless you specify, you get white. And most likely red isn't available even if that's what you prefer. If you like red chowder, come to Rhode Island.

By focusing on the story of chowder in one particular place, Rhode Island, I found that the past was not as rigid as we think. These are some of the rules I found:

"Don't be afraid of the onions"

"Never boil a potato in chowder."

"In the old day you could, if you wanted to, put in 'bout half a pint o' nice wine."

And from a man who had been cooking chowder for clam bakes in Rhode Island, not Manhattan, since the 1870's: "Put in a quart can o' tomatoes."

I can't say I was altogether surprised to read that the rules about chowder in the past were flexible, because things are no different today. You are much more likely to find Manhattan chowder in Rhode Island than in New York City, where New England chowder is the norm as it is just about everywhere. Many Rhode Island clam shacks offer a choice between red and white. A few add a third dishwater gray choice...variously called

Rhode Island or clear or plain (in a good way)...to the menu, but almost no place offers Rhode Island chowder exclusively, although you can probably find an old quahogger at every picnic table who will insist that there is only one way to make a chowder and that in Rhode Island we eat clear, plain chowder three meals a day.

The work before you contains a couple bowlfuls of history and quarts of the clam chowder that I ate when I spent a summer doing what many people only dream about: eating clam chowder every chance I had when it was chowder time up north.

*

Aunt Carrie's in Point Judith is a perfect place to start, because it offers all three classic clam chowders. And because it is almost one hundred years old. Like the lighthouse sittingly stolidly just behind the restaurant,

Aunt Carrie's is a leader not a follower.  To know what tradition is, rather than what people think it should be, come here.  The red chowder is daringly minimalist and unadorned. Nothing but clams and a few diced potatoes in a slightly sweet tomato broth.  Hot clamcakes take to it like fried potatoes to ketchup.  I almost burn my fingers swirling a fritter piece in the chowder, but my dunking action is bound to improve over the course of the summer.  Aunt Carrie's milk and clear chowders are fundamentally the same as the tomato, which makes comparing them especially easy.  These are neither thick nor thin chowders.  Their backbone comes from potatoes and not from flour.  The associations they bring to mind are musical as much as culinary.  So elemental and full of grace are these chowders that I feel as though I have tasted Shaker hymns, not soups.

# CHOWDER SUMMER

The Clamettes: 'Tis a gift to be simple, 'Tis a gift to be free, 'Tis a gift to come down to the sea.

Travelling Clamette: To see the sights!

Cooking Clamette: To buy fish straight from the docks!

Designing Clamette: To collect shells!

Big Sister Clamette: Kick up your leg, girls!

Those are my back-up singers, the Clamettes. They are four sisters and are figments of my imagination, but based on some special women in my family. In order of age, Big Sister Clamette, the quahog with a shell of gold, who keeps them all in line and in tune; then there's Travelling Clamette, a cherrystone who surfs the ocean currents to far off places; then there are the twin little necks, Cooking Clamette, a gourmet, and Designing

Clamette, with a flair for arranging flowers, furniture and songs.  You'll be hearing from them from time to time.

"Your New York side was coming out, Dave," a friend accused me when I mentioned that the first chowder of my chowder summer was a red one.  But, as you will see, it was my Rhode Island side that made me say, "I'll Take Manhattan."  Just as it is my Rhode Island side that prompts me to order New England clam chowder at three places in Newport.

If there is an epicenter of New England clam chowder it is around Bannister's Wharf in Newport. Here, the Clark Cooke House, The Black Pearl and The Mooring create a small triangle of milky white temptation.  All three are beautiful of face.  It's their hearts that are different.

The Clarke Cooke House is open and breezy, its

windows acting as frames for being looked as much as

for looking out and people watching. It has a zany, multi-

level design crammed with sailing bric-a-brac, set off by

naval bronze kept bright for the scrutiny of actual Navy

captains from the Naval War College nearby. The

chowder is positively yellow with butter melted in the

thin broth that cries out for thickening from the huge

oyster crackers served here alongside every bowl. Loads

of dill and the tenderest clams ever spooned complete

the seduction.

Eating at the Mooring is like entering a magazine

fashion spread with a Newport theme. The rooms are

large, warmly elegant and sparsely decorated with

models of sailing hulls and photos of classic yachts.

Maritime signal flags hanging outside spell something

whose code I imagine represents CHOWDER.

Designing Clamette:  I love the décor!

Imagine if velvet married silk and had a liquid child that was swathed in softest baby powder.  This would still be only a rough approximation of the smooth mouth feel of the white clam chowder at The Mooring.  They dust the top with a bit of Spanish paprika for a snap back to reality that then causes you to dip your spoon for another soothing mouthful of chowderized silk.

The Black Pearl Tavern is an institution.  In its dark and piratical interior I have been known to commit acts of utter abandon, like ordering a bowl of chowder and a burger together.  This is an abundant and sustaining chowder, brimming with clams and potatoes in a ramped up creamy Davy Jones' locker.  If the Tavern is too full, walk across the wharf to the Black Pearl Annex for a bowl from the takeout window.  Yes, this chowder

is so popular it needs an annex.  Try it with a hot dog
there, pirate.

 The Clamettes:  Beware the Newport Chowder
Triangle, you won't escape with your figure intact.

  Cooking Clamette:  Paprika, shake it, shake it,
shake it!

From *Baldwin's Monthly*, January 1875

*A Famous Rhode Island Chowder*

*Some of our old readers, says the* **Providence Journal***, will recall the late James Brown, a gentleman of genial and accomplished manners, some of whose social sayings have come down to the present generation, and shall not be gainsaid.  The following is his receipt for a chowder, very famous in his day, and not altogether forgotten in ours.*

*St. James' Chowder For Six*

*Take six slices of good pickled pork, (pig preferred,) and fry them in the bottom of a good-sized dinner pot, turning the slices till they are brown on both sides.  Take out the slices of pork, leaving the drippings in the pot.  Take seven pounds of tautaug, dressed, leaving* the heads on, or ten pounds of scup, (tautaug to be preferred,) and cut each in three pieces, unless small, when cut them in two. Place in the pot, on the drippings, as many piece of fish as will fairly cover the bottom of the pot. Throw into the pot, on the fish, three handfuls of onions, peeled and sliced in thin slices. Do not be afraid of the onions! Put in over this salt and pepper to taste, as in other soups. Then lay on the six slices of pork – on the top of the pork the rest of the fish; cover this with three handfuls more of onion, peeled and sliced. (Nine or ten onions in both layers will suffice, though more will not injure it.) More pepper and salt, to taste. Then pour into the pot water enough just to come fairly even with the whole, or partly cover the same. Put the cover on the pot, and place it on the fire. Let it boil gently and slowly for thirty minutes. It is to BOIL thirty minutes, not merely TO BE ON THE FIRE thirty minutes; and at all events, let it *boil until the onion is done soft. Pour in at this point about a quart (about a common bottle) of best cider or champagne, and a tumbler full of port wine, and at the same time add about two pounds of sea biscuits.*

*Note. – If when the onion is done, you find there is not liquor enough in the pot, soak the sea-biscuit in water for a few minutes before putting them in. I would recommend the practice generally.*

*After the cider, wine and crackers are put in; there is no harm in stirring the whole with a long spoon, though it is not necessary. Then let the whole boil again (not merely be over the fire) for about five minutes, and the chowder is ready for the table. Before dishing up let the cook taste it and see whether it lacks pepper or salt, when, if it does, it is a good time to add either.*

*NOTE. -- Also, never boil a potato in chowder. If*

*you want potatoes, boil them in a separate pot, and
serve in a separate dish on the table.*

*They make the "Rhode Island Chowder"
according to the receipt of the late venerable James
Brown, who, in his day and generation, was considered
the most accomplished chowder maker in the State, and
in whose honor was instituted the "St. James Chowder
Club," which boasts an antiquity of twenty-five years.*

The Clamettes:  We're not afraid of the onions!
We're not afraid of the Champagne!  Boil, chowder, boil!

Big Sis Clamette:  But I'm afraid of the fish with
their heads still on.  Cooking Clamette, why are you
crying?  Is it all the onions?

Cooking Clamette: No, it's because I've cooked
potatoes in the chowder all these years and like it that

way.

The Clamettes:  We're not afraid of the potatoes!  No separate bowl for the potatoes!

This recipe fascinates me for many reasons. First, because it presents chowder as it was initially cooked in its earliest days, as a layered dish, a sort of lasagna of the sea.  Here, a layer of fish is placed on the pork drippings, followed by a layer of onions, topped by salt pork slices, on which another layer of fish goes, then another layer of onions.  I'm also intrigued by the use of ship's biscuit as a thickener and the insistence that potatoes don't belong in the chowder.  Finally, who could resist a chowder in which a whole bottle of bubbly and a glass of port are key ingredients.

Here, at least, is a chowder recipe full of the kind of prickly commentary that accompanies so much contemporary discussion of chowder. But the rules

espoused by James Brown, the most accomplished

chowder maker of his day, have nothing to do with

whether the chowder is plain, red or creamy. To be sure,

this appears to be a separate genre of chowder

altogether. But Brown's stress is on the use of lots of

onions. So perhaps what made a Rhode Island chowder

in the old days was that it contained onions but not

potatoes. Wouldn't that confound those who consider

the modern day clear chowder with potatoes to be the

genuine historical article?

I longed to turn up some of the social sayings of

Mr. Brown for which he is famous in his day, but have

come up with nothing. Nor have I found any record of

the St. James Chowder Club. Was Mr. Brown the saint in

the club's name? Did his chowder warrant canonization?

Perhaps the club still exists and is a secret society, forced underground during the Prohibition era because of its addition of Champagne to the chowder. If so, I hope to be tapped for membership someday.

This is a good place to discuss a mini trend I've detected this summer. A few places are serving clams still in their shell in the chowder. This goes completely against the lasagna-layering, transformation of disparate elements into one through boiling, that is fundamental to chowder. I must admit, though, that these are two of the best chowders I have tasted.

At Local 121 in Providence, they are proud of their use of locally sourced ingredients. Things are so local here that my waiter (also a musician) lives right in the historic building, in housing for artists. He never has to go outside. I wonder if the apartments are as grand as the interior of the restaurant with its velvet-upholstered

banquettes, starched white tablecloths and paneled

walls. The chowder here is so home-made that even the

herb oyster crackers are baked in-house.

Crispy lardons float in the chowder, but not

diced clams. The clams are served on top of the

chowder, whole Matunuck clams in their shell. It is

pleasant to cradle a perfectly cooked whole littleneck

(sorry, Clamettes) in a spoonful of creamy chowder. One

of the problems with clam chowder in general is that

reheating makes the clams tough, and chowder is

frequently reheated. Local 121 never has a problem with

tough clams, but may have a problem with tough

traditionalists who expect their clams in, not on, the

chowder.

I have a similar chowder in New York City at a

new restaurant in the Village called The Clam.  The Clam

is one of the only places in New York City to serve

stuffies.  I invite a friend from Colorado to join me on this

chowder outing.  After the stuffies arrive, the waiter

returns with an empty bowl.  "This is for the shells," he

explains.   My companion, never having had a stuffie

before, seems to think it normal that you should have a

bowl to discard your stuffie shell rather than leaving it on

the perfectly good plate it arrived on.

"A plate with a couple of stuffies is not like a

bowl of mussels you need to excavate, leaving a pile of

shells in your wake," I say.

All becomes clear (to me anyway) when the

chowder arrives.  The chowder contains clams in the

shell so, of course, the bowl is for discarding those

chowder clam shells.  I think my poor friend feels as

confounded by all this shell etiquette as I would if faced

with a plate of Rocky Mountain oysters when visiting

him.

In 1878, the Continental Steamboat Company

bought Rocky Point, a coastal amusement park with the

largest dining room in the United States, world famous

for its clambakes . The park and the steamboats to reach

it and other points of interest along Narragansett Bay

cost the company $1,300,000. The steamer wars were

on, and the company's ship *What-Cheer* used to nose the

other boats out of the way at the pier to land its

passengers first. As a way to differentiate itself from the

competition, the company commissioned a guidebook.

*The Hand-Book of the Continental Steamboat Company*,

written by M.M. Whelan, was published in July 1882.

This little-known guide captures in amber the glory days

of the Rhode Island shore dinner, and is written in such a

charming fashion, that I have adapted several excerpts

from the text to contrast a chowder summer in 1882

with a similar journey today. And now, after a dose of

Count Rumford's Horsford's Acid Phosphate (one of the advertisers in the *Hand-Book*) for seasickness, let our voyage begin.

*Introductory*

*In presenting this modest brochure to the patrons of the Continental Steamboat Company, it is the intention to supply the needs of thousands of excursionists who desire to know just a little of the points of interest in swiftly passing up or down Narragansett Bay, and have not the advantage of sitting beside an old sailor or frequenter of the famous resorts which line the shores of this beautiful arm of the sea, extending inland twenty-eight miles from Point Judith to Providence. Imagine me, therefore, such experienced sailor, or at least an enthusiastic devotee of the pleasures of just such a trip as you are now taking, and we will, like the sailor, be only too happy to tell of delightful times had "down*

*river," of prodigious catches of fish, and of luscious clam-*

*bakes which will cause your mouth to water with*

*pleasurable anticipation. Should sufficient interest be*

*aroused by the brief mention of historical points, more*

*elaborate descriptions can readily be found in larger*

*guides and more ambitious works; but here we will*

*merely answers such questions as "What lighthouse is*

*that?" which will naturally arise; and we trust that we*

*will provide an agreeable compagnon de voyage.*

*Narragansett Bay*

*We are about to visit together another world, or*

*at least a new country, full of mysteries and unknown*

*delights, if you have never been there; and if you have, it*

*may give the pleasure of a "twice-told tale" to hear again*

*of a country which has a king, and a hundred thousand*

*willing subjects who are clamorous in his praise, who have voluntarily expended millions of money in his honor in palaces on sea and on shore; a king who has one of the fairest dominions of the earth, and yet has intellectual qualities of the lowest order, while his subjects are of the most intelligent class! What is there in common? There must be a bond of sympathy. Ah, yes; that king has a stomach, for which the human stomach has a wonderful affinity; and as the nearest way to a man's heart is through his stomach, all men love the clam.*

*Various pretenders have set themselves up in other places as the genuine King Clam of Rhode Island, and their ignominious failures were well deserved. Other clams are not happy, and have not the ability to impart happiness to others. They have a tough time of it among mud and rocks, and are tough themselves; but Rhode*

*Island clams have plenty of pure water, sandy beds of a peculiar softness, delicate shells, and even the foot with which it pushes itself along, which is commonly and erroneously called the neck of the clam, is tender and sweet.*

*Ah yes: we are slowly moving; and what a wonderful thing to see a great steamer like this quietly leave her dock without a scratch or a strain; yes, and without shouting and swearing, you will add.*

*"But what are those three shrill whistles," do you ask? That is the signal to the Superintendent of Point Street Bridge to open the draw. It is, as you see, a bridge of size, and there were many sighs at the size of the bills by the tax-payers of Providence before it was finally in order; but it is now an engineering triumph. It is a revolving bridge, and is operated by steam. You will see*

*the two openings now, -- the one on the right for*

*descending, and the one on the left for ascending vessels.*

*Our first landing is made at Field's Point, two and*

*three-quarter miles from Providence, where the veteran*

*Russ Fenner serves clambakes, as he has done for*

*seventeen years. Here a clam-dinner can be obtained*

*within the shortest possible time. There is a fine, sandy*

*beach for bathing upon the point, but its situation is*

*exposed. That quiet little cove just beyond, however, is*

*retired enough and received the name of Old Maids'*

*Cove, from their partiality for that secluded spot.*

*That thin boy assisting at the clambake is Bill*

*Crowell. He started here when he was eleven years old.*

*He's already very opinionated on the subject of clams.*

*Do you want to hear?*

*"Hello there, Bill! These damned*

*landlubbers...oh, excuse me, ladies, I am an old sailor after all...these fine passengers would like to know the secret to a good clambake?  What do you say?"*

*Bill shouts back, "You've got to have rockweed, and you have to scorch it!"*

*Well, there you have it.  Bill says a good bake requires the right seaweed to cover the clams.*

*What is that lighthouse?  It is called Sassafras Point Light, and is the first one we meet.  The next one is Fuller's Rocks.*

*But see, we turn our head now to the eastern shore, and the tasty buildings of the Squantum Club attract your attention.  You would like to join the club? Ah well, you must wait till someone dies, for their membership is full.  It is strictly a private club, and its property is isolated from the mainland. But no better dinner can be enjoyed by its aristocratic members than can be found in places open to everybody; and thanks to the Continental Steamboat Company, excursions are within the means of all. Right back of Squantum is Ocean Cottage, comprising some twenty acres of ground, a large part of which is a grove furnishing ample shade. Mr. C.J. Read is proprietor, and has accommodations for 25 permanent boarders, as well as for 300 shore dinners alone.*

*Silver Spring, almost adjoining Ocean Cottage, has a separate landing. It is now under the management of H.P. Bliss. His dining-hall, finely located on the rocky shore, can comfortably accommodate 600 people. The round building, on the edge of the rocks, is devoted to flying-horses, and there are numerous cottages on the bluffs which belong to Silver Spring.*

*What is that long pier? It is no wonder that you ask, and it is a sad story of financial disaster to some. Riverside Hotel was built ten years ago, by the Riverside Land Company, at a cost of over $40,000, and well furnished. The rooms are all large and high studded, and command a fine view; yet the hotel has never paid. The pier is 1,150 feet long, and cost over $50,000. For the past two years the house has not been open.*

*Leaving the pier at Riverside we take a southwesterly course by Sabine's Point Lighthouse towards Pawtuxet, and the river of that name, which supplies Providence with an abundance of excellent water.*

*Turning again sharply to the east we see Bullock's Pont, six miles from Providence, where Smith*

*Shaw keeps the "What Cheer House," and furnishes Shaw or shore dinners (whichever way you choose to spell it), of excellent quality to great numbers.  Around Bullock's Point are situated the famous oyster beds, which have given Providence River oysters such a reputation.  Just beyond is Nayatt, with its unused lighthouse.  The bay properly begins here, and widens to an expanse of nearly ten miles, and we can see the old towns of Warren and Bristol on the east shore.*

The biggest unsolved chowder mystery in Rhode Island is the origin of what one of my readers calls "orange chowder", which he says is not white or clear, but is also definitely not Manhattan.  The best known orange chowder was the one served at Rocky Point.  I think I solved the mystery, almost by accident.  You remember Bill Crowell, the boy we shouted to at Field's Point? Fifty years later, he's still at it, now master of the clambake at Crescent Park. He has grown up to be a lean follow with sharp cheekbones, intelligent close-set eyes and a walrus mustache. He wears a soft cap to protect his head from the sun, although it doesn't shield his protuberant ears. This is what Bill has to say about clam chowder, without which no clambake is complete:

"I don't make the chowder here. I'm a clam baker, and making the chowder is its own art. But I've seen enough of them I guess to know how it's done. Here's a recipe for a small group of a hundred people. First you'll need a wash boiler. Then take about two pounds of salt pork. Cut off all the rind, and slice it up thin. Slice it until it is all one mass of grease, almost like lard. Then try it out. Try it out in an iron kettle or pan—a frying pan will be all right. If there are any scraps left, take them out. Then you'll need a couple of quarts of onions. Chop 'em all fine, and when the fat is all tried out, put in the onions. Put in the onions and cook 'em in the fat, but don't burn 'em. Don't burn 'em!

Then you'll need about a peck and a half of potatoes—all cut in squares. Then put in a quart can o'tomatoes—'bout a pound of butter—little sage— pepper and salt 'n keep tasting of it.

The clams go in last of all. You'll need about five quarts of cut-out clams. Chop 'em all up fine, so there won't be any pieces any size at all. They go in last of all, as I said, and if there is any of the liquor—the juice—of the clams, put that in too.

The secret of a good chowder is in the onions. They say to me, how'd you do it, Bill, and I say, 'I d'know, I guess it's because I put onions in my chowder.'"

Bill lowers his voice. It's the Prohibition era after all.

"In the old days you could, if you wanted, put in 'bout half a pint o'nice wine—some kind o'nice wine. I d'know just what there was about it. For you couldn't taste it, but sort of gave the chowder a different taste. But we don't do it now."

Yes, a venerable veteran of fifty years of Rhode Island clambakes starting in the 1870's says that chowder should contain tomatoes. This is the chowder that Bill knew at the places he was closely associated with, Field's Point and Crescent Park.

But how did this orange chowder also make its way to Rocky Point for its apotheosis?

At an exhibit of Rocky Point Park artifacts at the Warwick Public Library, presented as part of the annual Quahogger's Jamboree there, I noticed an old advertisement for the park. Below a notice for the daring aerial exploits of the Six Flying Herberts, and in only slightly smaller print, the advertisement touted "Shore Dinners, 12-6:30 daily. Served by Chas. E. Lyon."

Eureka! In the 1926 *Providence Journal* profile of Bill Crowell from which the conversation and recipe above are drawn, Bill is photographed with Charles E. Lyon, who is identified as a senior member of the firm at Crescent Park. The article says that Mr. Lyon also worked at Field's Point in the old days. I believe this is evidence that there was a direct chowder pipeline (via Bill and Charles) from Field's Point to Crescent Park and to Rocky Point, and the chowder flowing through it was orange.

There is one thing missing from Bill's clam chowder recipe, however, and that is the crackers used as a thickener. Rocky Point's president Conrad Ferla confirmed to journalist Carol McCabe in 1975 that unsalted Seacoast crackers were dissolved in the chowder to make it thicker. Perhaps the crackers also contributed to the orange tone.

Bill Crowell died on July 10, 1948 at the age of ninety-five. He worked at Crescent Park until its dining hall was destroyed in the 1938 hurricane. When Bill retired in 1940, he estimated that his shore dinners had been eaten by more than eight

million people.

Nothing stays the same in New York City, but Manhattan clam chowder clings to life there in one stubborn spot, at the intersection of 42nd Street and Vanderbilt Avenue. At the Grand Central Oyster Bar, Manhattan and New England clam chowders are both on the menu, and from my usual Friday night perch at the counter overlooking the tureens from which the servers themselves draw the chowder, I watch as roughly three bowls of New England are served for every bowl of Manhattan.

You could once walk through a tunnel from Grand Central to the Yale Club of New York City, but nowadays a jaunt across Vanderbilt Avenue is required. One muddles through somehow. On days that the Tap Room has its seafood buffet, Manhattan clam chowder relives its glory days, and one sip transports me to the days of F. Scott Fitzgerald and cotillions in the ballroom.

Those "splendid hours", and Manhattan clam chowder's own era of greatness, have passed.

Ed's Chowder House in New York City is nothing like its name suggests. It's not the little clam shack on the East River you might assume, but a fine restaurant by Lincoln Center. Ed's offers a chowder sampler, with New England, Manhattan and corn. Just when I'm beginning to think maybe Manhattan clam chowder is more vibrant in New York than I thought, I realize that this is Manhattan blue crab, not clam, chowder. I like the idea of a sampler like this, though. It's the restaurant equivalent of a chowder cookoff. In this case it was a draw. My favorite here is the bread basket, holding old-fashioned corn sticks, still warm.

Those corn sticks remind me to discuss chowder accompaniments. Sure, there are the oyster crackers. A friend of mine refers to one particular brand as the "good" oyster crackers and he is very disappointed when another brand is served.  Perhaps this is why he takes my unused crackers home with him for later use whenever we go clam shacking, because my sack of crackers as a rule goes unopened, unless it is a thin and brothy chowder that could stand some stiffening.

I will not, however, pass on homemade oyster crackers, particularly if they are seasoned with herbs. I'm not sure if the huge oyster crackers at the Clarke Cooke House in Newport are homemade (I haven't been able to find them commercially), but those are so similar to the ship's biscuit of chowder yore that I feel I could subsist on them.

Popovers also taste great with chowder!  That eggy airiness cries out for a dip in some hot New England chowder. This I discovered at a restaurant called

Popovers in Epping, New Hampshire, where the creamy

chowder is made from freshly shucked clams and where

they will be happy to fill a popover with lobster salad for

you, which is another idea whose time has come.

Clamcakes, of course, are the ultimate

accompaniment to clam chowder of any variety. It's a

wonder to me that no one has thought of serving micro-

clamcakes that can be stirred directly into the chowder

like oyster crackers. But I suppose, the pleasure comes

from dipping a bit of the hot crispy fritter into the

chowder to have the contrast of crispy and soggy.

The restaurant Blu in East Greenwich may have

gone too far, however. Blu's chowder and clamcakes

combo presents such a small crock of chowder with the

clamcakes that the chowder becomes more of a

clamcake dip than the proud co-equal it deserves to be.

Finally, a note about hot sauce.  Yes, I've seen the bottle of hot sauce on the counter at the Black Pearl Annex's take out window, and I met a man at a local farmer's market who stirs a dash or two of that fire water into every bowl of chowder before taking a sip. That man sells homemade salsa at the market.  For my own tastebuds, hot sauce is for stuffies, black pepper is for chowder.

*Hand-Book of the Continental Steamboat Company*, continued

*We must now turn our attention once more to the western side, and here we can see the identical place where the "Gaspee" was burnt, on the 10th of June, 1772. This was in reality the second overt act which led to the Revolutionary War,--the first being the sinking of the "Liberty," in Newport harbor, in 1769. Conimicut Point Light is next  passed, and we steer in a southwesterly direction straight for Rocky Point, views of the chief places of interest in which will be found interspersed through this work.*

*The first object to attract your attention is a massive bronze lion, fastened to a rock, which children delight to mount and sit upon. The next is the little field-piece used to salute the steamers as they approach.*

*Then comes the Band Stand and Police Headquarters,*

*new this year.  Then the Ladies' Reception Room, and,*

*right in front, the Fountain, from which pure water can*

*be drawn from ten faucets.  We will now ascend the*

*Tower, 160 feet above the level of the sea, from which a*

*magnificent view can be obtained of all the country*

*round.  The extent of the grounds, 100 acres, more than*

*twice as large as Boston Common, can here be noted, as*

*can the variety of hill and dale, rocks and ramble, grove*

*and meadow, and peaceful farm of which it is composed.*

*Looking out across the Bay you can see Patience,--not the*

*comic opera, but the island of that name;--also Prudence*

*and Hope and Despair.  Jutting out into the Bay is*

*Warwick Neck, crowned with delightful villas.  Sweeping*

*around Warwick Lighthouse, we can see the charming*

*Greenwich Bay, and then a series of green hills and fertile*

*farms till we arrive again at a view of the water.  No one should leave Rocky Point without a visit to the Tower; but*

*so we can say of all its numerous attractions, a mere*

*catalogue of which would be quite extensive.*

*Perhaps the most fascinating of all is the*

*immense Cage of Monkeys, where their amusing pranks*

*are an endless source of enjoyment to little people and,*

*we fancy, too, to those of larger growth.*

*Let's at least mention the Coliseum, where*

*vaudeville entertainments are given every afternoon, and*

*the tent of Indians making baskets for sale, the Glass*

*Blowers with their fragile wares, the Punch and Judy*

*Show, the Ice Cream and Refreshment Room, the Bowling*

*Alleys and the Skating Rink. But the greatest attraction*

*of all, next to its natural beauties, is yet to be mentioned.*

*The Ocean House, overlooking the water, has a*

*dining-room capable of seating 2,000 at one time, and at*

which 5,000 have been furnished with shore dinners in a single day.  On the occasion of the visit of President Hayes to this hotel, 250 bushels of clams were consumed at one meal.  It is the largest room in the United States for dining purposes.  A view of its long tables, with stiff, white napkins and bright silver-ware, set for large company, is a rare sight of order and neatness.  A view after the repast is one of confusion worse confounded. But let us witness the preparation.  A hot fire, made of hickory sticks, is snapping and cracking as its flames rush up the chimney erected over the platform of stones upon which the fire is built.  Smooth, round stones placed between the pieces of wood become red-hot with the heat.  When all is burned, the ashes are swept away, and clams, corn, and other vegetables are piled upon the stones and covered with seaweed.  A bucket of water and a sailcloth to keep in the steam is added, and the clams *are let to cook.*

*A clam dinner consists, first, of baked clams; second; of clam chowder; third, of baked clams; fourth, of fish chowder; fifth, of baked clams; sixth, of fried fish; seventh, of baked clams; eighth, of clam fritters; ninth, of baked clams; tenth, of baked fish; eleventh, of baked clams; twelfth, of sweet potatoes; thirteenth, of baked clams; fourteenth, of sweet corn; fifteenth, of baked clams; sixteenth, of raw tomatoes; seventeenth of baked clams; eighteenth, of cucumbers; nineteenth, of baked clams; twentieth, of lobster; twenty-first of baked clams; twenty-second, of watermelon; twenty-third, of baked clams; twenty-fourth of clam-cakes; twenty-fifth, of baked clams. If you wish any more clams baked, you are at liberty to speak to the waiter. No wonder everyone leaves a Rocky-Point dinner with a self-satisfied air, and walks to the boat with head erect. It is impossible for*

*him to stoop over. As he leaves the boat, you can see*

*written all over him the words, "I have dined today."*

I love this only slightly exaggerated description

of the utter gluttony and abandon of a proper clam feast.

We all know that there are people in this world who do

not have enough to eat. We also may learn in the most

painful way possible that there are people who, because

of illness, cannot eat, and whose chief fixation is food.

As my father wasted away from lung cancer while I was

eating away for this book (he was unable to swallow

because of the tumor and was fed for months through a

feeding tube), how I longed to see him eat a meal of such

munificence and plenty as a Rhode Island shore dinner.

But that was not what he craved. He confided in me one

day that all he could think about eating was sardines and

crackers. "And the funny thing is, I never even liked sardines," he mused.

Many clamshacks allow you to replicate the kinds of multi-course clam feasts perfected by Rocky Point. For example, at Monahan's at the Pier in Narragansett, I help celebrate a left-coast friend's homecoming with clamcakes and cups of New England chowder, followed by boxes of fried whole belly clams and fried scallops. "Those are some bellies." my friend comments. He means the fried clams, but he could have been talking about the ones straining our belts.

At Rocky Point Clam Shack, an homage to the old amusement park in a ramped up trailer that has made a very welcome appearance in a parking lot on Post Road in Warwick, a few miles away from the real Rocky Point, the primal need to be clam-sated once in a while is indulged.  They serve a dish called the Palladium,

consisting of two boiled lobsters, steamers, Central Falls

kielbasa, corn on the cob, fries, watermelon and

chowder.  They get a lot right at the Rocky Point Clam

Shack, not least of which is rekindling people's emotions

about food.

And I notice something curious about the Rocky

Point Clam Shack.  People tend to sit looking out at the

Post Road traffic, rather than towards the trailer where

the food is cooked and where all the action is, including

old signs, vehicles and props from the park's now

demolished attractions.  It mystifies me why they are all

looking in the wrong direction as they eat their orange

chowder and clamcakes.  Then it hits me.  They are

facing the Bay, orienting themselves to true Rocky Point,

even as they enjoy its spirit somewhere else.

In early September, 1944, a period when the park had been closed for several years when trade dropped off during World War II, the bronze lion at Rocky Point that children delighted to sit on for more than sixty years (fondly known as Leo the Rocky Point Lion) was destroyed by vandals. His back had been broken, his tail snapped in two, and his remains found scattered across the road—except his head, which was believed to have been thrown into the bay. Heavy tools were required to so thoroughly destroy this gentle creature.

Sometimes, when I am walking along the water at Rocky Point today, I think I hear him roar.

I taste a couple of rare chowders. My friend Ed, the Evel Knievel daredevil of quahog cookery, invites me onto his sailboat to prove that clamcakes and chowder can be made from scratch at sea, or at least secured by lines at the slip, on a 28 foot sailboat. Ed looks completely relaxed in his Hawaiian shirt, and hardly appears to be working as we sip his home brewed ale and chat. The table is set with a blue and green striped table cloth and  enamel bowls labeled "catch of the day" that I know will soon be filled with chowder. A cooler brims with eggs, lettuce, celery, onions, potatoes, clams. He pulls out a container with our first course, snail salad, made from whelks, tomatoes and olives that he serves atop a wedge of iceberg lettuce. Quahogs simmer on the two burner cooktop and open up in no time. Ed sautés bacon, then adds to the hot fat celery and onion that he has brought to the boat pre-diced. After they are soft he adds the clam broth that the quahogs cooked in to the pan, along with clams he has chopped without my even noticing, diced potatoes and, yes, tomatoes.

As the chowder cooks, he mixes a clamcake batter which, like the best clamcake makers, he fixes without reference to measuring cups. It took him many attempts in his early days of clamcake cookery to get his mixture of flour, eggs, baking powder and clams just right, but now he has it down. But can he do it on the sailboat? He has placed the fryolator in the boat's sink for safety, in case of any rocking from the wake (we are at the very end of the pier). I am allowed to taste the first clamcake, and it is crispy perfection, and perhaps the fullest of clams I have ever tasted. With perfect timing, Ed's wife join us from work just as the best clamcake and chowder lunch I have every had at sea is served.

The chowder made on Trolley Day in Chepachet, however, may be the rarest of all, since it is only served every hundred years.  On Sunday, June 29, 2014, one of the most unique chowder events of the last century occurred.  The Chepachet Union Church re-enacted the day the town first welcomed the trolley to town a hundred years before by serving the same lunch of chowder, clamcakes and watermelon that was served in 1914.  I always love the food that is made by church volunteers.  Plus you can't beat the prices.  On the big day, I arrive early in hopes of chatting up the volunteers to learn the secrets of their recipes.  Signs everywhere in red, white and blue announce, "Trolley Day Combo! Chowder, 3 Clam Cakes, Watermelon $7 *Drinks for sale at the Youth Booth).  A blow up of a photo the first

Trolley Day is displayed in a tent along with a piece of the original Chepachet Trolley rail, which people approach like a relic of the true cross.

I don't manage to talk my way into the kitchen, but I spy some straw-bonneted ladies (attendees were encouraged to wear period clothes) bring out pots of chowder from the church hall and transfer it to chafing dishes. I see big pieces of salt pork pulled from the chowder. A good sign. The men are charge of the clamcakes in the corner and I watch, salivating, as they hazard a few trial attempts to make sure the oil in the deep fryer is hot enough. I am temporarily diverted from the food by a parade of vintage cars passing the church grounds. But finally the food is ready and I queue up to learn the really burning question. What kind of chowder will it be? I can't hold it in any longer. It is red. A volunteer assures me that this was the color of the

chowder a hundred years previously too. I deem it too

zealous to demand proof.

From the old photo, it looks like there were a lot

more picnic tables around in 1914. I eat my meal cross-

legged on the grass. Were there this many flies buzzing

in 1914? The chowder is excellent, but I have to eat it

quickly because the public addresses are starting. The

blessing is interrupted by a bunch of Hell's Angels roaring

past. That part is unscripted, but is taken in stride, with

a lot of mumbling all around that that didn't happen in

1914. Then comes an historian's talk about the

importance of the trolley coming to town. If any part of

Rhode Island is remote, this is it. The day before the

trolley arrived it took five hours to get to Providence by

stagecoach or horse and buggy. The trolley cut the time

down to fifty-five minutes.  The most pertinent fact I

learn is that the trolley was also used to transport goods,

including clams and other fresh seafood to Chepachet.

Chepachet's own great export that made the reverse trip

was ice.  Clams, ice and a trolley to carry them, a match

made in heaven, and all the more reason to celebrate

the Trolley's arrival to town with a clamcake and

chowder lunch.

*Handbook of the Continental Steamboat Company*, continued

*So we approach Block Island.  Its numerous hotels, noticeably the Ocean View, appear in sight, and we can see the long breakwater stretching out its arm to hold back the force of sea.  Competition is very lively between the hotels for the patronage of the transient excursionists, and employment is given to runners and "dodgers" by the thousand to bring in custom.  You are importuned to favor with your presence a dozen hotels, and are impressed with your importance the minute you land.  There are two things that are conspicuously absent, roads and trees.*

These days, there are roads on Block Island. There have to be for the mopeds that annoy the residents.  With my mother and stepfather (who were married here on the Mohegan Bluffs) I make a visit every summer, and our day is invariably the same. On the verandah of the Shining-esque Spring House hotel, we have a New England chowder with crispy bacon sprinkled on top and savor one of the most sweeping views of the Atlantic available in Rhode Island. As an excuse to linger, we order lobster and corn fritters absolutely bursting open with both fillings like such rich man's clamcakes should. You get a sense from dishes like this that Block Island hotels are still striving to impress us with our importance and to lure us from the ferry.

After such indulgence, a trip (on our mopeds, of course) to the Poor Man's Pub is in order for the best stuffed quahog on the island. We stop at the state beach for a swim in water of Aegean clarity, then finish the day with a bowl of chowder at the National Hotel in the center of town.  This is one of those chowders in which the celery sweetly strikes the prominent note.

Even though you can see Montauk, New York from here, you won't see much Manhattan chowder, or clear for that matter.  Even at the popular Bethany's Airport Diner, where a lot of New Yorker's fly into, the award winning Ma's Homemade Chowda on the menu is "New England style with plenty of clams."

Before leaving, I fill my lungs with the sea air perfumed with beach roses, close my eyes and face the sun, preserving this day and its chowders, swimming and heat for recall come February if I should need it.

Travelling Clamette:  I'm going to get married here someday, on the bluff, to a guy who's sweet, not gruff.

The Clamettes:  Ooh, ooh, she's getting married

here, that's right.  The dress and the chowder will both

be white!

And now for some Olde Time Rhode Island chowder humor.

Big Sis Clamette:  In other words, stuff that only David laughs at.

On May 5, 1907, the *Providence Sunday Journal* published a poem called "The Origin of Clam Chowder" by Frederick Moxon, a man who was so obsessed by chowder that he invented a legend about its creation and then set it in elegant and humorous verse.  He seems to have been influenced by those scamps, the adolescent authors of *The Tale of the Clam*, which appeared a few decades earlier and purported to explain the origins of the clambake.  Clearly, we have nothing

better to do in Rhode Island than write historical poems
and trilogies about seafood.  According to Moxon, clam
chowder was invented when Chippitoxie, the beautiful
daughter of the chief of the Narragansett, promised her
hand to the man who brought her the "the newest
fashioned feast of most delicious flavor."  This turned
out to be chowder, and its discoverer was another
Narragansett, Pettaclamscutt, famed for fishing, who
one day unearthed a clam with his fishing spear:

Digging up a dozen others,

Fast he sped to his own wigman;

Built a fire and cooked them quickly

Hastened them to Chippitoxie,

Who already in the doorway

Sniffed the precious feast approaching.

At the first delicious mouthful,

Kind she smiled on Pettaclamscutt;

At the second, sighed relenting;

At the third made full surrender

And was won by Pettaclamscutt.


Then her papa Wockamansett

Having likewise tried the flavor,

With a grunt of satisfaction

Gave the happy pair his blessing,

And full sanction for betrothal.

# CHOWDER SUMMER

Now was made great preparation

For a marriage and a feasting

Such as never yet was heard of

In the tribe of Narragansett.

And the skill of Chippitoxie

So prepared the new found shellfish

That the thousand guests assembled

Made great "Chow-chow" of the matter,

And the dish was christened "Chow-der."

This example of Chowder humor appeared in the "Editor's Drawer" section of *Harper's New Monthly Magazine* in February 1865:

*General H and Colonel R were popular members*

*of the Rhode Island Bar. General H had been the popular*

*Chief Justice of our Supreme Court.  Colonel R was one of*

*the most brilliant men of his day -- the Sheridan of the*

*legal profession.  A Rhode Island clam-bake and chowder*

*is a State Institution.  In the mysteries of the chowder*

*these gentlemen were unequaled as experts; there*

*existed a generous rivalry; each had his partisans.  A*

*pleasant party had assembled to test the relative powers*

*of General H and Colonel R. Each exceeded his previous*

*effort; the crowd was fed; the verdict of the boys*

*unanimous in favor of General H, Colonel R asked*

*consent to propose a toast to his successful competitor.*

*He said a few words as only he could say and look such*

*things and proposed the health of General H, "The Great*

*Chowder Head of Rhode Island!"*

Big Sis Clamette:  That one should have stayed in

the editor's drawer, where it belonged.

An article titled "Around Cape Cod" from the British publication *Hunt's Yachting Magazine* (May 1, 1869) revealed both the fame of Rocky Point chowder and the notion that chowder wasn't for everyone:

*Monday morning found us on deck bright and early, getting everything in order, preparatory to taking our lady friends to Rocky Point, a famous place for picnics and chowder parties. The Rhodes [sic] Islanders say this is the place for a chowder, as Rhode Island is the favored spot where we find the finest clams in creation. At 9h.30m. a.m. we started with a light air on our teeth, and in an hour of so were becalmed, but as we were in such good company we did not complain, yet we were not sorry when a light puff or two carried us into the anchorage. Luckily for the writer of these lines, who does not believe in such conglomerations as chowder, it was*

*as the waiter said, "all out"; Anglice – gone, eaten up,*

*devoured, however other eatables were available and we*

*had a very efficient beef, mutton and other meats.*

Now that Rocky Point has been "all out" of chowder for a couple of decades, it is even more disappointing to read that this Nineteenth century sailing party didn't get to have any. Something similar happened to me and a friend at the Whistle Stop restaurant in Albion. They were all out of chowder the day we visited, and I haven't since had a chance to return. Unlike, the British sailors, I was not happy when the waiter said "all out." Their chowder is said to be excellent. Fortunately, fried scallops were available.

"They All Ate Clams" boasted the headline of an article in the proceedings of the American Electric

Railways Association (Volume VII) about a Rhode Island Company outing held on Saturday, July 27, 1919 on the grounds of the Warwick Club. "There a luncheon of chowder and fried eels was served and each man was given his fill of this delicious Hoover food." I don't know what's funnier, the term "Hoover Food" or the serving of fried eels with the chowder, although the fact that Americans were implored to eat less wheat and fat (two critical ingredients of clamcakes) during and after World War I in order to send food to the hungry of Europe is likely the very earnest reason for this unconventional combination

The St. Michael's Clam Bake, a "church bake" attended by many members of the prominent DeWolfe family of Bristol, inspired Bishop M.A. DeWolfe Howe to pen a witty ditty in 1864, which ingeniously seems to use the names of every parishioner at some point.  This

excerpt about the chowder is a delight, and calls

attention to the fact that proceeds of the bake would be

used to build St. Michael's Chapel :

Our matronly church is much in the lurch

For a place to encradle her lambs;

So play we the old trick—a jolly pic-nic—

And a love feast of chowder and clams.

....

Here comes Mr. Waldron bringing fish from the cauldron

And clams reeking hot from the sea-weed;

While Carpenter Lawless, axe, gimlet and saw-less,

Offers chowder as fast as we need.

I, for one, wish I had been a member of clever

Bishop DeWolfe's flock.

And now a self interview with the author, because it's my favorite way of determining what I really think.

DNS:  Is that it?  Didn't you eat any more chowder?

DNS:  Yes, there were other chowders, some of them excellent, but the ones described above were my favorites or were worthy of discussion for other reasons.

DNS:  Don't be stingy.  Talk about a few more. Tell the readers about the day you went on a chowder crawl to five different clamshacks.

DNS:  Did you have to bring that up?  My stomach has only started to recover.  A couple of friends and I started in Watch Hill and ended in Galilee.  I had a clear chowder at St. Clare's Annex in Watch Hill that was actually more golden than clear, and which makes sense given the wealth of Watch Hill. Then in Misquamicut, at the Seafood Haven, I had a bowl of the creamy New England chowder, with one of the sweetest bases I came across. It almost reminded me of corn chowder. The Hitching Post Restaurant, in that "in between" stretch of Route One that cries out for a clam fritter pit-stop, had a pungent Rhode Island chowder that could deliver a knock-out punch to any other claimant to that title. Next came the Matunuck Oyster Bar where the three of us on this crawl shared a cup of white chowder that rivaled The Mooring's in smoothness. Finally, my last cup was literally that, a Solo paper cup of tangy red/orange, at the Port Side in Galilee.

DNS: Do you have any advice for those who might want to go on a crawl of their own?

DNS:  Bring your own extra disposable bowls and spoons for sharing.  We were constantly short of one or the other and clamshacks often charge you extra for them.

DNS:  You haven't said.  What is your favorite kind of chowder?  White, red, clear…or orange?

DNS:  I like a white chowder that is milky rather than creamy.  I call the thick New England variety "chowder on a spoon" because of the way a plastic spoon will stand up in the middle of it.  You can find my favorite type of white chowder at the Clarke Cooke House in Newport, Tommy's Clam Shack in Warwick and Howard's Chowder Shack in North Scituate.

DNS:  So you have now written about clamcakes in *Clamcake Summer*, stuffed quahogs in *Stuffie Summer* and chowder in *Chowder Summer*.  Are you done with clams?

DNS:  I'm finished with writing about them, I think, but never with eating them.  But I'm surprised that you haven't recognized that these works have only superficially been about clams?

DNS:  If not clams, what are they about?

DNS:  Nostalgia, for one.  And homesickness.  I started this project when I bought a house in Rhode Island after years of living elsewhere.  But I can finally say that I've eaten enough of the foods that I missed to now truly believe I am home.

*Champagne bottles pop, confetti rains from above, while the Clamettes dance me out.*

See you in the summer, friends.

# ABOUT THE AUTHOR

David Norton Stone was born in Providence, Rhode Island. He is the author of *Trial of Honor: A Novel of a Court-Martial* and the three titles in the Rhode Island Quahog Trilogy: *Clamcake Summer*, *Stuffie Summer* and *Chowder Summer*. He a graduate of Bishop Hendricken High School, Yale and The University of Connecticut School of Law.

www.ingramcontent.com/pod-product-compliance
Lightning Source LLC
Chambersburg PA
CBHW060345050426
42449CB00011B/2831